I'D FOLLOW "THE WAY" IF I COULD SEE THE ROAD MORE CLEARLY!

Seeing Jesus' Story Through New Lenses

Bob Gardenhire III

The scriptures are offered from two sources. The NIV First-Century Study Bible is my favorite translation. The Message Bible is my favorite para-translation i.e. the author offers a close translation from the original sources and tries to put it in everyday language for his readers.

ACKNOWLEDGMENTS

The journey of bringing this book to life has been one of collaboration, dedication, and creative effort, and I am deeply grateful to those who have played a role in its completion.

First, thanks to my wife, Annette, who wholeheartedly supported the writing of this book. You gave valuable feedback on its content and form. As always, you have generously lent me your computer skills in formatting and organizing this book.

I am blessed to have wonderful, spiritually minded friends with whom I have had multiple conversations over the years about the tenets of this book. Thanks especially to Rev. Dr. Bill Crowell. Your love of Creation Spirituality has woven its way into the themes of this book. Thanks to Dr. Curt Gruel, Co-Director of HeartPaths Oklahoma City. Your keen theological insights, coupled with your love of Jesus, have always helped me not only enjoy my journey with God but also clarify many of the points expressed in this book. Many thanks also to Butch Barnett, my hairstylist. Butch, you listen to many stories every day and hear your clients' questions about life and God. The conversations we have had, reflecting on what people question or believe about God, along with your own insightful questions, have helped my ideas gain clarity and evolve.

Beyond personal conversations that shaped this book, I am also deeply grateful to the professionals who helped bring it to life.

I owe so much to the dedicated team at Book Publishing Plus (BPPLUS) for their unwavering encouragement and professional support throughout the publishing journey. Thank you, Aaron Wilson, for your enthusiastic energy and knowledge of the publishing process. As the first person I spoke with when exploring self-publishing, you convinced me without a doubt that BPPLUS was the right choice for me. That has proven true!

I have a wealth of gratitude and esteem for my Project Manager, Kevin Paul. Your genuine concern for my book has been a steadfast encouragement. You have a great listening ear and have responded to all my requests and questions with helpful professional knowledge and suggestions.

Thanks also to the entire BPPLUS team! My sincere appreciation goes to James Horn, whose editorial expertise and keen eye have helped refine and shape this manuscript. Your thoughtful guidance and meticulous work have been invaluable. The fact that what I wrote has made an impact on you means so much to me.

I extend my gratitude to Kofi for the beautiful illustrations that add depth and meaning to these pages.

Your artistic talent has enriched this book in ways that words alone could not.

Lastly, to my readers—thank you for your support and for being a part of this experience. I hope this book resonates with you and enriches your own journey with God.

Bob Gardenhire III

Contents

PREFACE

In his book *Say Yes*, Scott Erikson shares his wife's real-life experience. She had taken their kids to the Portland Zoo on a hot summer day. They were standing at the large window, looking into the African lions' quarters. The lions were sleeping. While standing there, she overheard another mom explaining something to her kids who were also at the lions' quarters. She said (to one of her kids who had asked a question), "Well, honey, these lions don't have manes because, uh, it is hot out and they, uh, shave the lions' manes to keep them cool in the summer."

Upon hearing this explanation, Scott's wife turned to the other mom and offered kindly and gently the true facts of the situation. "These lions are female. They don't grow manes." Embarrassed, the lady thanked her, took her kids, and moved on to another exhibit.

When Scott's wife related this story, he thought to himself, "What if my wife had not been there?"

What if, like the other mom and her kids above, we have been told stories or received explanations from trusted sources that actually were misinformation? We, too, might believe many things that we think are true and factual but aren't. I believe we all have added things to our "truth file" that, in actuality, are not true or accurate.

1

We each have been and are impacted by our families, trusted others, cultures, learning environments, web info, and myriad other sources of information.

Across the 50+ years of my professional life, I have listened to the stories of thousands of people. As a chaplain, pastoral counselor, minister, therapist, and spiritual director in the Christian tradition, I have accompanied these people as they lived out their faith amidst what life had brought them. Often, they struggled to find comfort in beliefs that, in the light of their circumstances, were somehow brought into question.

I, too, as a person who follows the way of Jesus, have spent most of my life in a quest for the key concepts and truths of my Christian faith. I have dedicated my life to serving Jesus and have diligently sought to grow in my understanding of that faith story and to mature into the kind of person God has designed me to be and hopes I will be. In my journey, I have had many mentors. I have listened to teachers, professors, authors, and preachers. I have given myself to be a lifelong learner. I have learned from studying scripture and tradition and listening to my own reasoning and experiences. Through those and other avenues, *I have been given a story* that isn't the "traditional story" many Christians have been taught. Many of the people I have learned from speak of this rediscovered story as 'alternate orthodoxy.'

The impetus for writing this book comes from knowing that the alternate story, which I now believe is the more accurate story, is not readily found in our Bible Belt, including Oklahoma, nor in many Christian churches. I listen to many people these days whom God is inviting to move out of the traditional Jesus story into seeing him with new eyes. This book will help them understand what the rediscovered story is about and also help them develop a plan on what to read and study next to keep growing their faith. I am writing this book so my kids and grandkids can explore the different story if they choose. In the vein of what Scott Erikson said, "What if, for my kids and grandkids, I fail to tell the story that has been coming to life in me in these many years?" It may be that they won't hear it from other sources in their lives. So, I write this book. I will present the truth as it has come to me. I also believe that this book could help someone who has been turned off by certain Christian groups and their beliefs, and consider this new vision of who Jesus is and how to follow in his way.

Blessings,

Bob Gardenhire III.

PART ONE

Above all, let's get this straight: those who follow "the way" of Jesus know that GOD IS UNCONDITIONAL LOVE!

God is not vindictive or revengeful or the bearer of retribution. God is always working to RESTORE the world and its people to their best selves, their divine image and likeness. Therefore, if we are to live out of the divine image and embody God's likeness, we will be about love. We will be about restorative, redeeming love.

God's Everlasting Love

"I have loved you with an everlasting love; I have drawn you with unfailing kindness" Jeremiah 31:3 NIV First-Century Study Bible.

"I've never quit loving you and never will. Expect love, love, and more love" Jeremiah 31:3 The Message Bible.

What Does God Want?

"God has shown you, O Mortal, what is good. And what does the Lord require of you? To act justly and to love mercy and to walk humbly with your God" Micah 6:8 First-Century Study Bible.

"But God's already made it plain how to live, what to do, what God is looking for in men and women. It's quite simple: Do what is fair and just to your neighbor, be compassionate and loyal in your love, and don't take yourself too seriously—take God seriously" Micah 6:8 The Message Bible.

The Greatest Commandment

"Teacher, which is the greatest commandment in the Law? Jesus replied, 'Love the Lord your God with all your heart and with all your soul and with all your mind.' This is the first and greatest commandment. And the second is like it: 'Love your neighbor as yourself.' All the Law and the Prophets hang on these two commandments" Matthew 22:36-40 NIV First-Century Study Bible.

"'Teacher, which command in God's Law is the most important?' Jesus said, 'Love the Lord your God with all your passion and prayer and intelligence.' This is the most important, the first on any list. But there is a second to set alongside of it: 'Love others as well as yourself.' These two commands are pegs, everything in God's Law and the Prophets hangs from them" Matthew 22:36-40 The Message Bible.

God Is Love!

"Dear friends, let us love one another, for love comes from God. Everyone who loves has been born of God and knows God. Whoever does not love does not know God, because God is love" I John 4:7-8 NIV First-Century Study Bible.

"My beloved friends, let us continue to love each other since love comes from God. Everyone who loves is born of God and experiences a relationship with God. The person who refuses to love doesn't know the first thing about God, because God is love" I John 4:7-8 The Message Bible.

Love Is Indispensable

"If I speak in the tongues of humankind or angels, but do not have love, I am only a resounding gong or a clanging cymbal. If I have the gift of prophecy and can fathom all mysteries and all knowledge, and if I have a faith that can move mountains, but do not have love, I am nothing. If I give all I possess to the poor and give my body to hardship that I may boast, but do not have love, I gain nothing" I Corinthians 13:1-3 NIV First-Century Study Bible.

"If I speak with human eloquence and angelic ecstasy but don't love, I'm nothing but the creaking of a rusty gate. If I speak God's Word with power, revealing all God's mysteries and making everything plain as day, and if I have faith that says to a mountain, "jump," and it jumps, but I don't have love, I'm nothing. If I give everything I own to the poor and even go to the stake to be burned as a martyr, but I don't love, I've gotten nowhere. So, no matter what I say, what I believe, and what I do, I'm bankrupt without love" I Corinthians 13:1-3 The Message Bible.

Imitating Christ' s Humility

"Therefore, if you have any encouragement from being united with Christ, if any comfort from his love, if any common sharing in the Spirit, if any tenderness and compassion, then make my joy complete by being like minded, having the same love, being one in spirit and of one mind. Do nothing out of selfish ambition or vain conceit. Rather, in humility value others above yourselves, not looking to your own interests but each of you to the interests of others. In your relationships with one another, have the same mindset as Christ Jesus; who, being in very nature, God, did not consider equality with God something to be used to his own advantage; rather, he made himself nothing by taking the very nature of a servant, being made in human likeness. And being found in appearance a human he humbled himself becoming obedient to death—even death on a cross!" Philippians 2:1-8 NIV First-Century Study Bible.

"If you've gotten anything at all out of following Christ, if his love has made any difference in your life, if being in a community of the Spirit means anything to you, if you have a heart, if you care—then do me a favor: Agree with each other, love each other, be deep-spirited friends. Don't push your way to the front, don't sweet talk your way to the top. Put yourself aside, and help others get ahead. Don't be obsessed with getting your advantage. Forget yourselves long enough to lend a helping hand. Think of yourselves the way Christ Jesus thought of himself. He had equal status with God but didn't think so much of himself that he had to cling to the advantage of that status no matter what. Not at all. When the time came, he set aside the privileges of deity and took on the status of a slave, became human! Having become human, he stayed human. It was an incredible humbling process. He didn't claim special privileges. Instead, he lived a selfless obedient life and the died a selfless, obedient death—and the worst kind of death at that—a crucifixion" Philippians 2:1-8 The Message Bible.

Summary

The "heart of the matter" for a follower of the way of Jesus is love. Love over faith. Love over beliefs. Love over knowledge. Love is the beginning and the end. Yes, faith is very important. Yes, hope keeps love alive. But to live in God and become like God is to become a person who loves. For Jesus, right actions speak louder than right beliefs, for if one doesn't become transformed by love to be loving, what you believe really doesn't matter. Remember, we will explore many themes and issues in this book, but the heart of the matter is LOVE!

Some Readings on Love

If love is the soul of Christian existence, it must be at the heart of every other Christian value. Then, for example,

Justice without love is legalism;

Faith without love is ideology;

Hope without love is self-centeredness;

Forgiveness without love is self-abusement;

Fortitude without love is recklessness;

Generosity without love is extravagance;

Care without love is mere duty;

Fidelity without love is servitude.

"Every virtue is an expression of love. No virtue is really a virtue unless it is permeated or informed by love," Richard Rohr.

"...the love of God is unlike anything else in creation. We use the English word 'love' a lot. We love our family or closest friends, but we can also love tacos, a particular color, and our favorite sports team. There's only one English word for all of it. But the love of God throughout the Old and New Testaments is talked about in very particular language that is not used for anything else.

"The Hebrew word, *chesed,* and the Greek word *agape* are used to talk about the holy, unique love of God that is more like a never-ending commitment than a feeling of affection. Neither word describes action born from duty-bound obligation or resentment. The commitment of *chesed* or *agape* love is not mandated by any outside force. Instead, it is driven by a selflessness that leads this one who loves to voluntarily do what no one has the right to expect or ask," Rev. Michaele Lavigne, *Changed In The Waiting: An Advent Devotional,* pp33.

***

Pierre Teilhard de Chardin asserted that love is the most powerful force in the universe. For Teilhard, "Love is the most universal, the most tremendous and the most mysterious of the cosmic forces."[1] Love is both human and divine. Divine love is the energy that brought the universe into being and binds it together. Human love is the energy that drives whatever we do (for the divine) to keep ourselves and our world growing together in unity and peace.

***

"Love, which might be called the attraction of all things toward all things, is a universal language and underlying energy that keeps showing itself despite our best efforts to resist it. It is so simple that it is hard to teach in words, yet we all know it when we see it. After all, there is not a Native, Hindu, Buddhist, Jewish, Islamic, or Christian way of loving. There is not a Methodist, Lutheran, or Orthodox way of running a soup kitchen. There is not a gay or straight way of being faithful, nor a

---

[1] Louis M. Savary and Patricia H. Berne, *Teilhard De Chardin On Love: Evolving Human Relationships,* pp. 3.

Black or Caucasian way of hoping. We all know positive flow when we see it, and we all know resistance and coldness when we feel it. All the rest are mere labels," Richard Rohr, *The Universal Christ.*

***

"What religion do I preach? The religion of love—the law of kindness brought to light by the gospel. What is this good for? To make all who receive it enjoy God and themselves, and to make them, like God, lovers of all," John Wesley.

Part Two
Lenses Through Which to See and Understand God-Jesus-Spirit

Some Lenses to Help You Focus

When I go to my ophthalmologist appointment twice a year, they always check to see if my glasses are the right strength for the best eyesight. With my glasses off, I cover my left eye and try to read the descending size lines on the chart on the wall. Then, I cover my right eye and do the same. Lastly, I do the same drill with my glasses on.

Eventually, they have me look through a lens machine. First, the right eye. Looking at the chart, the technician starts adjusting. The tech says, "Which is clearer, one or two, as the filters are brought to bear?" I go through a series of one-two choices until I have the clearest vision possible. Then, I switch eyes and go through the same routine. At the end, the tech compares the filters with the current strength of my glasses' lenses. In this way we discover if my glasses are still viable or whether I need a new prescription.

The following section of this book will offer several lenses that have helped me see/discover a truer picture of Jesus' story and teachings. These lenses will hopefully be like the accurate information that the woman at the zoo offered the mother who had told her kids that they had shaved the lions' mane to make them cooler. After this section on "lenses to help focus," I will offer my story of Jesus and his mission and what I believe he teaches and how to follow his way.

Lens #1 : Our Limited Ability to Know

1 Corinthians 13:12, "For now we see only a reflection, as in a mirror, but then we will see face to face. Now I know only in part; then I will know fully, even as I have been fully known" (NIV First-Century Study Bible).

"We don't yet see things clearly. We're squinting in a fog, peering through a mist. But it won't be long before the weather clears and the sun shines bright! We'll see it all then, see it all as clearly as God sees us, knowing him directly just as he knows us!" The Message Bible.

Every year, as the director of the HeartPaths Training Program in Spiritual Direction, I had the opportunity to meet with prospective students about our program. If they were truly interested in applying for inclusion, I would ask them a few questions to further ascertain their "fit and congruence" for our program. I asked them if they could keep absolute confidentiality. I asked them if the time of the class worked for them and could they see themselves attending at least 80% of the sessions. I asked them if the tuition was affordable. I asked them if they could "be still" as the class would be practicing different kinds of prayers together and quiet was necessary. Then, I would ask them if they could be tolerant of others who believed differently than they did. I explained that since we are an ecumenical training center (i.e., open to various faith backgrounds and denominations), it was often the case that the group might have broad spectrums of belief about Christian faith and practice.

Almost all of our applicants would say they could grant tolerance. Then I would push it a little bit further and ask, "Do you know all there is to know about God, yes or no?"

I never had anyone say they did! I would then quote Paul's statement in 1 Corinthians 13:12, telling them that since we don't know all about God, the tolerance we required was not just a tolerance based on their personal compassion or magnanimity but rather on the humility that none of us knows the whole truth about God. Even though we hold our beliefs with passion, we might be right OR wrong.

So, in this book, I will be relating the truth about God that I have come to believe. I might be right; I might be wrong. Nevertheless, I offer these ideas because I believe they are worthy of consideration.

Lens #2 : How We View the Bible Lenses

There are several aspects to this lens that help us appreciate and revere the Bible rather than worship the Bible. The Bible is our sacred story. It contains the evolving wisdom, history, and guideposts that help us develop our relationship and journey with God. The Bible is still being written.

A. The Bible Is Not God's Word

   1. As the noted Christian author C.S. Lewis wrote in a letter to Mrs Johnson on November 8th, 1952: "It is Christ himself, not the Bible, who is the true word of God. The Bible, read in the right spirit and with the guidance of good teachers will bring us to Him. When it becomes really necessary (i.e. for our spiritual life not for controversy or curiosity) to know whether a particular passage is rightly translated or is MYTH (but of course Myth specially chosen by God from among countless myths to carry a spiritual truth) or HISTORY, we shall no doubt be guided to the right answer. But we must not use the Bible (our fathers too often did) as a sort of encyclopedia out of which texts (isolated from their context and not read without attention to the whole nature and purport of that book in which they occur) can be taken for use as weapons."

2. John's Gospel says that Jesus is the Word. "In the beginning was the Word, and the Word was with God, and the Word was God. He was with God in the beginning. Through him all things were made; without him nothing was made that has been made. In him was life, and that life was the light of all mankind. The light shines in the darkness, and the darkness has not overcome it" (John 1: 1-5 NIV First-Century Study Bible).

   "The Word was first, the Word present in God, God present in the Word. The Word was God, in readiness for God from day one. Everything was created through Him; nothing- not one thing came into being without him. What came into existence was Life, and the Life was light to live by. The Life-Light blazed out of the darkness, the darkness couldn't put it out" (The Message Bible John 1:1-5).

B. Jesus' Perspective on Scripture
   1. "You study the scriptures because you think that in them you have eternal life. These are the very scriptures that testify about me, yet you refuse to come to me to have life" (John 5:39-40 NIV First-Century Study Bible).

      "You have your heads in your Bibles constantly because you think you'll find eternal life there. But you miss the forest for the trees. These scriptures are all about me! And here I am, standing right before you, and you aren't willing to receive from me the life you say you want" (John 5:39-40 The Message Bible).

I think what Jesus is pointing to is that our relationship with him is possible and that it is what brings us life. Knowledge of scripture is good. A relationship with Jesus is better. We'll look at this in more detail in Part Three.

2   Jesus, as a rabbi/teacher, came from a tradition of "midrash." The word "midrash" comes from the Hebrew root "drash," which means to seek, inquire, or investigate. This method involves critically interpreting and explaining scripture to reveal layers or insight that expand far beyond the literal meaning (Peshat) of the word on the page to explore what the text might suggest or imply (Derash). Midrash was/is a way of reading scripture that acknowledges that every generation needs to interpret scripture according to their place in time and development. Rabbis of each generation would interpret the texts in light of their current situation. Then, they would record these interpretations in the Talmud. The Talmud was a collection of previous generations' interpretations.

As Sandy Eisenberg Sasso writes in her book, *God's Echo: Exploring Scripture With Midrash*: "The Rabbis, writing between 400 and 1200 C.E. filled in the gaps through midrash. Grounding themselves in the biblical narrative, they retold the ancient story in light of new realities and changing conditions. Through this interpretative method they made sense of contradictions in the text, provided missing information, and made the narrative relevant to the times in which they were living."

This means that for Jesus, scripture was dynamic. The meanings might change from generation to generation. For example, Jesus would say, "You have heard it said...but I say to you." He was updating the midrash of prior generations. He also found ways to interpret the deeper meanings of scripture. For example, when the leaders wanted to stone the woman caught in adultery, he said, "Let he who is without sin cast the first stone." At another time, he reinterpreted the belief of doing no work on the Sabbath by healing a man on the Sabbath.

C. The Language Jesus Spoke

Most likely, all the scriptures you have read have been in English. The ancient words, across the years, have been translated from many different languages and cultures. This has led us to miss the nuances of the words written and spoken in the Bible we now have. Neil Douglas-Klotz has devoted his life to "re-planting" the scriptures in the language used by Jesus and those around him, i.e., Aramaic. He writes: "The richness of expression present in the Aramaic language of Jesus is a treasure that has been lost...to discover this treasure we must challenge ourselves to participate in the prophetic mystical tradition that Jesus represented....According to native Middle Eastern mysticism...each Aramaic word presents several possible 'literal' translations. 'Blessed are the meek, for they shall inherit the earth' could easily be translated, 'Blessed are the gentle' or 'Blessed are those who have softened the rigidity within'" (from *Prayers of the Cosmos,* Neil Douglas-Klotz, page 1).

So, what we have inherited in our sacred scriptures has come from Aramaic and Hebraic languages being translated into Greek and Roman languages and on and on into English. The vibrancy, essences, and nuances have often been lost. One of the most striking and consequential misquotes I have run across has been the words found in John 3:16. The words we most often have read say, "whoever believes in him shall not perish but have everlasting life" (NIV: First-

Century Study Bible). In one of his lectures, Neil Douglas-Klotz says that the most accurate translation of the word "IN" from the Aramaic is not "in" but "LIKE." What a tremendous change in meaning. It's not our dogma but our lived beliefs and behavior that we are called to embody. "Whoever believes like him shall not perish!"

D. The Non-Literal Bible

Noted biblical scholar Marcus Borg stated in his book *Speaking Christian* that the two main hindrances that keep people from fully understanding the heart of Christianity are reading the Bible literally and believing the key paradigm of the faith is the Heaven-Hell paradigm. Let's look at the literal or non-literal issue first.

In another of his books, *Reading The Bible Again For The First Time*, Marcus Borg makes these observations about the differences between a literalist and a non-literalist approach to reading the Bible.

1. Origins. Literalists believe the Bible was written by God. Non-literalists see it as written by the faith communities of Israel and the Early Christian movement. For non-literalists, it is a human response to their experience of God.

2. Authority. Literalists believe that since God wrote the scriptures, they are authoritative

and true. Non-literalists see it as sacred because it is the witness of faith across the years.

3   Interpretations. Literalists see the Bible as historically and factually true. The events really happened as recorded. Non-literalists interpret the Bible as a sacrament, i.e., a means of grace and a place where God is present as we read and digest it.

4   Characteristics.

   i.   For literalists, the Bible is: 1. Literally true, 2. Doctrinal, 3. Moralistic, i.e., good as seen through a sin/guilt/forgiveness lens, 4. Patriarchal, 5. Exclusivistic, i.e., Jesus as the only way to salvation, and 6. After-life oriented.

   ii. Non-Literal Christians see the Bible as a lens through which to see and encounter God and as a sacrament through which the Holy Spirit deepens one's relationship with the divine.

NOTE: Christians sometimes say, "This is what the Bible clearly says!" Given lenses 1 and 2, the non-literalist's perspective would be, "This is my interpretation of what the Bible says."

Lens #3 : What Do We Mean When We Say, "It's God's Will?

It was God's will! That's a phrase often used by Christians to mark events or outcomes. However, the myriad of ways it's used can sometimes be confusing. Consider these categories of meaning;

1. *Everything happens for a reason.* It seems to me that a better way to say that is, "Every action has a cause." There are things that happen to us that God did not will or want to happen, e.g., traumas, abuse, murder, to name a few. More often than not, we must glean meaning out of things that happen for ourselves.

2. *God is in control of everything.* Again, there are many things that happen that God does not want to happen. God may eventually use everything for a good purpose and certainly wants us to overcome adversity for our betterment. To say this another way, God is never the author of evil or punishment for the sake of punishment or learning.

3. The Old Testament book of Deuteronomy taught that if bad things are happening to us, it's because we broke the law and/or sinned. If you are prospering, it means that you are being rewarded for faithfulness to God or your behavior. (The

book of Job was written to challenge the Deuteronomic Code. Job's friends kept trying to get him to confess that he had sinned even though he hadn't).

My understanding of the meanings of the phrase "It's God's Will" came through one of my experiences as a chaplain at Hillcrest Medical Center in Tulsa, OK, in the early 1970s. It is one thing to learn theology in seminary classes, it is quite another to learn from real-life experience.

I was the hospital on-call chaplain one weekend. As was often the case, I got a call late one night from the ICU nurses requesting a chaplain's help. A 25-year-old man had been admitted into ICU following a brain aneurysm. I responded. He was in critical condition. He was hooked up to every lifesaving machine available. To be honest, he was probably dead even as they put him in the respirator. However, it took several days to let the process unfold.

His family soon began to arrive. I was present in the ICU waiting room and greeted each family member as they came in. It was a large family, and, over the course of a day or two, some 40 of his family came to keep vigil. With that big a family, my weekend was mostly dedicated to that ICU waiting room. As the family members hunkered down, I could hear their conversations. About half the family members were talking about, "We just can't question this; God has a plan, we have to have faith."

The other half of the family was expressing things like, "How could this happen? What kind of God would allow this? He spent two tours in Vietnam without a scratch, how could he have had this happen while he was washing his car? This isn't FAIR!"

Over the weekend, these two factions would have their spats. They were approaching this event from two different perspectives. My role was to provide spiritual care for everyone there. Needless to say, it was a challenge. For instance, how do you pray with two different "camps?" How do you keep your own beliefs and perspectives out of the equation? I was perplexed. I didn't exactly know what I believed and the skill of blending with these differing views took all I had in me.

Monday morning, I corralled Chaplain Patrick, the head of the chaplain's department and supervisor. He ushered me into his office and my story poured out. What he heard was that my inner turmoil was not allowing me to be present with all the family members. He said he thought that if I addressed my issues, I would be a better chaplain to them. Then he turned around, picked up a book out of his bookshelf and gave it to me. "Read this, and then let's talk again."

The book he handed me was *The Will of God* by Leslie Weatherhead. In a few words, here's the jist of the book. Weatherhead was the senior minister at a big church in London, England, during the WWII years. One morning, after a night of bombing by the Germans, he was walking down the street past some bombed-out buildings. In one of them, dead bodies were visible, including the bodies of several children. He passed two people and overheard one of them say, "We can't question this; it was God's will." He was deeply upset by that statement. He believed that God does not cause tragedies. So, he set out in his church sermons to address the situation. He preached six sermons on the will of God and how to understand it. Those sermons became the precious book Chaplain Patrick had given me.

Weatherhead preached that we use the phrase 'the will of God' too loosely. He preached that we need to understand that there are different meanings to that phrase. One meaning is God's intentional will, i.e., what God desires for us. The second meaning is God's circumstantial will, i.e., what God allows, given human freedom and the laws of nature. The third meaning is God's ultimate will, i.e., what God is working for that will come about later. From that perspective, deaths from bombings are not God's intention but only what God allows. And in the midst of that reality, God is working to bring about the ultimate goodness God would have wanted in the first place.

Reading that book gave me an internal place to stand with that family and any crisis in general. It reminded me of what God had spoken to me when my grandfather died: "Bobby, I don't like it that your grandad died either but you are going to be alright!" That book has been foundational to my own theological reasoning. It helped me be able to minister better and undergirded my belief that God doesn't cause tragedies. I have shared that book with hundreds of people and mention it here for you also. To me, it is the Gospel truth.

Introduction to Lenses 4-7 : Moving on From the Heaven-Hell Paradigm

We now turn to the second statement of hindrances that have dominated Christian understanding, i.e., the heaven-hell scenario. In traditional Christianity, the storyline is encapsulated in several scripture stories. First, the Adam and Eve story has been interpreted as establishing the fall of humankind, hence, human nature has been changed into something separate from God, embodying evil. This is passed down to each new generation. (Lens 4 will address this.)

Second, if we are evil, we are destined to hell unless something or someone saves us. (Lens 5 will address this.)

Third, theologians then deemed that God needed a perfect sacrifice to forgive and redeem us. This perfect sacrifice would take our place for the punishment we deserved. This substitutionary sacrifice would pay our debt and save us. (Lens 6 will address this.)

Fourth, the Cross then becomes the way God saves us since Jesus takes our place as the perfect sacrifice. (Lens #7 will address this.)

Lens #4 : Reinterpreting the Adam and Eve Myth

The story of Adam and Eve is a mythic story that explains why life is so hard and the consequences of disobeying the commandment not to eat from the Tree of the Knowledge of Good and Evil. It led to the idea of "original sin." The specific doctrine of "original sin" was developed in the 3rd-century struggles against Gnosticism by Irenaeus of Lyons and was shaped significantly by Augustine of Hippo (354-430 AD), who was the first author to use the phrase "original sin." Influenced by Augustine, the Council of Carthage (411-418AD) and the Second Council of Orange (529 AD) brought theological speculation about original sin into the official lexicon of the church. Eventually, the church, calling the sin of Adam and Eve "the Fall," created the idea that human nature wasn't even capable of choosing good but was forever corrupted.

Think About This

When God decided to give humans free will, God knew it would give us the capacity to make good and bad decisions. Surely, God understood that we would not be able to be "perfect" in our decisions and actions. God was not naïve. God made us in God's image, which includes the freedom to make choices. So, why would God punish us so severely for making a mistake, especially the first mistake?

Yes, there is always a first "no" to following God's way. There is always, for each of us, that first time. However, just as a loving parent would teach a child and perhaps set consequences, God would also respond. A loving parent would not banish their child from all grace or forgiveness. They would give their child a chance to learn and do better.

Moreover, as we will see in Lens #5, God would not cast us into eternal fire for making a mistake or even a series of mistakes. That would, by human standards, be cruel and unusual punishment. To go further from a midrash perspective, consider this from Rabbi Harold Kushner. He interprets the Adam and Eve myth very differently. In his book *How Good Do We Have To Be,* Kushner says: "I believe that the essential message of religion is a liberating message, not a restricting or punitive one. I believe that the fundamental message of religion is not that we are sinners because we are not perfect, but that the challenge of being human is so complex that God knows better than to expect perfection from us.

"I will be offering a radically different interpretation of Adam and Eve, one that will permit us to think better of God and to think better of our first human ancestors as well….To say that we are destined to lose God's love or go to Hell because of our sins is not a statement about us but about God, about the tentative nature of God's love and the conditional nature of God's forgiveness."

(And, of course, we have seen in Part One that God's love is everlasting and unconditional.)

A corollary consequence of interpreting the Adam and Eve myth as changing the nature of human beings was also added by early Christian theologions, i.e., Adam and Eve's catastrophic sin not only led to expulsion from the garden and changed their DNA it also brought DEATH into the world. Consequently death becomes an enemy to be defeated.

Think About This

To say that Adam and Eve's sin brought death into the world means that before they ate the apple they were immortal. One contemporary theologian calls their pre sin condition "conditional immortality."

Boy howdy, to me that misses the mark by quite a long ways. The constructive and destructive forces of life and nature somehow work together to keep life alive. Both are needed. So, yes, we don't like things and people we love to die, but it is a part of accepting the nature of things.

To check out my thinking I emailed my mentor and friend, Dr. Louis Savary, one of the world's foremost scholars on the evolutionary spirituality of Pierre Teilhard de Chardin, the Jesuit theologian. I asked him what evolutionary science would say to that interpretation of Adam and Eve. Here's what he wrote back, "Even before our solar system was started, the universe experienced suffering, death, and birth. Stars either died out or blew up as novas or were devoured by black holes. Astronomers estimate that a new star is born in the universe every three minutes. From what we know about the evolving history of our planet, suffering and death have been part of it for three billion years before homo sapiens ever appeared. The earth 'suffered' earthquakes, tsunamis, ice ages, etc. With the advent of plant life, insect life, sea life, and animal life, we have suffering and death as an integral part of evolutionary life. As for sin and the sources of sin (the seven deadly sin sources), most of the animals, especially the higher apes, knew pride, greed, envy, lust, sloth and gluttony. They were "sinning" long before humans discovered sin."

Another corollary consequence of interpreting the Adam and Eve story as "the fall" is that we have looked at humans since then as unworthy of God's love. If we are evil then we are unworthy. This has led to traditional Christianity to look at humans as shameful beings. We have lost our belief in original righteousness i.e. we are created (still) in the image and likeness of God. We are not perfect and might feel embarrassed at our own behavior at times but our core self is still in the image and likeness of God.

The power of shame leads us to the lie that we are unworthy of God. Let me say it clearly, God's love for us is not about our worth, rather our worth is about God loving us. We aren't perfect but we are loved. As I heard it said colloquially on time, "Our pictures are on God's refrigerator."

NOTE: If you want to learn more about how shame affects our relationship with God I heartily suggest you read, *God's Unconditional Love* by Wilkie and Noreen Au. It is a powerful book to set your free from shame. Moreover, if you are down on yourself because of shame, please listen to the song "*You Say*" by Lauren Daigle.

You are beloved
you always have been,
even before you were born.

You are beloved
you always will be
forever and ever, eternally.

You are beloved
right now, this very second
you are dwelling in God's love.

You are beloved
evcry cell and molecule
is bathed in nourishing love.

You are beloved
with every breath you take---
inspiring in you, Godly love.

You are beloved
not only when you are aware,
but when you've turned away.

You are beloved
not only on the mountaintop,
but in your desert wandering.

You are beloved
not only in your exuberant joy,
but in your anguished suffering.

You are beloved
by our God who knows you
wholly, fully, completely.

You are beloved
by our God who sees all you do,
and all the colors of your heart.

You are beloved
by our God who sends angels
protecting, encouraging you.

You are beloved
by our God who is life, light, love-
revealed to all, in the Christ.

You are beloved
because God has created you
and all God creates resides in Love.

You are beloved
by the One who is beyond creation,
and so you will always be beloved.

Lens #5 : God Is at Least as Good as the Best of Humankind and More

My Seminary Experience

Dr. Taylor McConnell, a professor of Christian Education and my first advisor at Garrett Theological Seminary, said those words, which have stuck with me as a guiding principle ever since. I like the way my friend, the Rev. David Ottsen, put it in the following poem.

He led the reflection groups in which all first-year students had to participate. The groups aimed to teach us to reflect on our seminary experience. Weekly, we would meet and share our key experiences from the preceding week. I had never been a part of such a group; it taught me the importance of reflection in learning. That group foreshadowed what I would learn down the road in my clinical pastoral education training. It taught me that God was at work in our lives, and we only had to reflect on experiences to glean the gifts of the Spirit at work.

God is at least as good as the best of humankind and more! God is always acting for the highest good possible. God always acts out of unconditional love and grace. We are called to as well!

That statement fits beautifully with beliefs I had fashioned in my growing-up years. I declared my intention to be a minister when I was fourteen years old. I felt God calling me to serve in that way. I had felt God's love and compassion during my grandfather's long battle with emphysema, and I wanted to able to provide the care that represented God's presence. (One of my high school classmates also declared his intention, but his motivation was to preach the hellfire and brimstone message of his tradition. I hated that style of religion.) It wasn't any wonder to me then that the immediate result of hearing that statement from Dr. McConnell was to validate my belief that God was not a "hell fire and brimstone God" out to punish for every foible and sin. For me, the concept of hell as punishment never made sense.

My Chaplain's Experience

Little did I know that two years later, I would take a year off from seminary to pursue advanced chaplain training at Hillcrest Medical Center in Tulsa, Oklahoma. During that intensive year, I was assigned a series of duties on various floors in the hospital. They wanted us to experience how different illnesses and conditions could affect people. One of those assignments was to be a chaplain at the Burn Center for three months. It was an incredible and harrowing experience. The excruciating pain of not only the burns but also the treatment of debriding the burnt skin was unbelievable. Not even the strongest dose of painkiller could curb the level of pain suffered. If a human being were to cast someone into eternal burning, we would consider it cruel and evil. Certainly, if in our goodness, we would not condemn someone to eternal flames, neither would a good God. (What does that tell us about Christians across the centuries burning people at the stake? Such a misguided travesty.)

A Perspective from Paul R. Smith

In his book *Integral Christianity,* Rev. Paul R. Smith writes this about hell: "Jesus talked about Hell (Gehenna) more than anyone else in the Bible (11 out of 12 mentions). However, we have changed from Jesus' use of the word to outlandish and oppressive meanings. Note the following facts about hell from Jesus' viewpoint as recorded in the New Testament gospels.

1. Jesus never, not once, connected hell with whether one was a Christian or not. He never connected it with anyone's religion.
2. In every instance, Jesus connected hell with being unloving, not with being unbelieving.
3. Hell was Jesus' radical commentary on those who oppress others in the world here and now.

4. There are over 30 passages in the New Testament that say no one will be left behind in any kind of eternal hell because everyone will be ultimately brought into eternity with God" (*Integral Christianity,* pp.254). For the above passages and a fuller explanation, see Paul's booklet *Hell? No!,* a Bible study on why no one will be left behind. That booklet can be found at Paul's website: revpaulsmith.com.

Do you wonder if God is the author of tragedy and suffering? If you use the maxim that Dr. McConnell taught, it can offer a lens to see that God is not cruel and would never desire us to have such pain and suffering as a punishment.

Hell, No! So what happens to us then after we die? Knowing that entire books has been written on this topic alone, I offer these thoughts that work for me.

The Franciscan medieval scholar, Bonaventure represents the Alternate Orthodoxy viewpoint that as our contemporary, Rob Bell says, "Love Wins," i.e., all will be saved. As Richard Rohr writes in his book *Eager To Love,* "much of the language of medieval times in the Christian tradition was about fire and brimstone, worthy and unworthy, sin, guilt, merit and demerit, justification and atonement, that has taken over in the last five centuries, when you read Bonaventure, you will find little or none of that. His vision is positive, mystic, cosmic, intimately relational, and largely concerned with cleaning the lens of our perception" (*Eager To Love*, pp162ff).

Bonaventure's vision had three great truths that held everything together for him. Emanation-everything comes forth from God bearing the divine image. Exemplarism- everything at the core is an example of the character and creativity of its creator. Consummation-we return to the source from which we came and this is God's supreme and final victory. (*Eager To Love*, pp166.)

As St. Paul put it "God has made known to us the mystery of his will, according to his good pleasure that he set forth in Christ, as a plan for the fullness of time, to gather up all things in him, things in heaven and things on earth. (Ephesians 1:9-10 NRSV)

Great! But what about all the evil people? Do they get to return to God as well? That's where the rubber meets the road, isn't it. Can we believe in the full power of God's restorative work? Can we possibly enter the mind of Jesus who in his suffering at the hands of evil powers and misguided people said, "Father, forgive them for they know not what they do?" It just doesn't sit well does it. After all we want those who do mean and dastardly things to get what they deserve. I know I do. I know how long it took me to forgive the two boys who bullied me when I was a kid and that isn't even close to what others have suffered at the hands of evil ones. I know sometimes I am called to go beyond myself and that I must rely on the Holy Spirit to help me do that.

Here are some perspectives that have helped me be ready to even consider forgiving the truly evil deeds that some people do.

1. Years ago a journalist who had spent over 20 years in the Middle East was interviewed about his experiences. At one point the interviewer said, "Why is it that a peace accord cannot be reached in the Middle East?" The journalist answered, "Because they hate their enemies more than they love their own children!" Instead of forgiving the past they keep repeating it. That's what revenge and retribution do isn't it! Revenge and retribution just keep the vicious cycle going.

2. William Paul Young's book, *The Shack*, paints a striking picture of God as one who is in the restoration business. The story is about the journey of Mack as he lives with the awful tragedy of his six year old daughter being kidnapped and killed. At the end of the book Papa (God) asks Mack to forgive the man who killed his daughter in the sense of releasing him to Papa so that Papa can deal with him. When Mack wonders how in the world to do that Papa says that level of forgiveness only comes through my presence in the one forgiving. Papa also says, "give him over to me so that my love can burn from him every vestige of corruption."

3. The idea of one's corruption' being burned away reminds me of the caterpillar and the butterfly. When it's time for the developmental transition to happen, the

caterpillar builds a cocoon and enters a liminal time until the transformation is complete and it comes out of the cocoon a butterfly. My understanding is that in the cocoon the caterpillar is dissolved and reconstructed as a butterfly. What if that is what happens to all of us in the transition beyond this life into the next? What if all that is not godly, whether miniscule or huge, is dissolved and the image of God in us is all that is resurrected and goes home to God? If that is true then the evil does not return to God.

Those perspectives have helped me wrap my mind around the issue of the afterlife, i.e., that state of being that is all love and light. I hope God will help you through these perspectives and others to find peace in this issue of afterlife. One thing for sure as Papa said, "forgiveness only comes through my presence in you."

Lens #6 : Reinterpreting the Abraham and Isaac Story

The story of Abraham and Isaac (Genesis 22) is often viewed as either a litmus test for one's faith and obedience to God and/or as a foreshadowing of how Jesus would be the sacrificial perfect one who would expiate all of our sins.

The Hebrew people had developed a sacrificial system that required offering up a "perfect" animal sacrifice (e.g., burnt offerings of bulls, rams, goats, lambs, doves, and pigeons). Moreover, many of the ancient religions practiced live human sacrifice to appease the gods/God. No wonder it has been interpreted as stated above.

If you take the story of Adam and Eve and see it as a story of how humankind's nature was changed and became depraved and then couple it with the Abraham & Isaac story, is it any wonder that the idea arose that God needed a perfect sacrifice in order to forgive us? Hence, the need for Jesus to be that perfect sacrifice. ("He died for our sins.")

BUT what if we understood the Abraham & Isaac story as actually opposed to the practice of sacrifice? William Paul Young, in a lecture given at the Trinity Conference at the Center for Contemplation and Action, presents such an alternative understanding. Since the ancient religious world was so steeped in perfect sacrifices, the Abraham & Isaac story starts out in that frame of reference so as to pique the reader/hearer's interest—but contrary to the prevailing understanding, it makes the surprising point that God does not want sacrifices at all. God will provide communion and forgiveness not because of a perfect sacrifice but because God's nature is always seeking restoration!

Here are some Old Testament scriptures that express that viewpoint and declare that God hates human sacrifices.

Leviticus 18:21: Do not give any of your children to be sacrificed to Molek, for you must not profane the name of your God. I am the Lord.

Deuteronomy 12:31: You must not worship the Lord your God in their way, because in worshipping their gods, they do all kinds of detestable things the Lord hates. They even burn their sons and daughters in the fire as sacrifices to their gods.

II Kings 21:6: He sacrificed his own son in the fire, practiced divination, sought omens, and consulted mediums and spiritists. He did much evil in the eyes of the Lord, arousing his anger.

Isaiah 1:11: The multitude of your sacrifices—what are they to me. Says the Lord, "I have more than enough of burnt offerings, of rams and the fat of fattened animals: I have no pleasure in the blood of bulls and lambs and goats."

Hosea 6:6: For I desire mercy, not sacrifice, and acknowledgement of God not burnt offerings.

(All scriptures from the NIV: First-Century Study Bible)

So, if God did not need a perfect sacrifice to forgive us and save us from hell, what then is the meaning of the Cross? Lens #7 will address that question.

Lens #7 : The Meaning of the Cross

Given the reinterpretation of the Adam and Eve and Abraham & Isaac stories, it follows that God did not require Jesus, the perfect one, to be sacrificed SO THAT GOD COULD FORGIVE US. That version understands Jesus to be the substitutionary atonement for our restoration to God and salvation from the fires of hell.

Make no mistake, however, forgiveness does entail a sacrifice. In forgiving, we sacrifice or forfeit our need for revenge or retribution. And we have seen that revenge and retribution are not the character of our Christian God. Rather than revenge and retribution, our God is a God of restoration and redemption.

So, Jesus' sacrificial death is not needed in order for God to forgive us, but it is a sign that God has already forgiven us. Yes, Jesus' death is a sacrificial atonement. No, Jesus' death is not a substitutionary atonement.

I have always believed this, but I had to know the details of what I believed. The following statement, *The Alchemy of Love,* declares how I currently understand Jesus' death and how you can understand it too!

The Alchemy of Love: Reflections on the Meaning of the Cross

Embracing Suffering

In the hit television series *Kung Fu*, which aired from 1972-1975, actor David Carradine starred as Kwai Chang Caine, a Shaolin monk who came to the American West in search of his half-brother, Danny Caine. All the episodes included flashbacks to his growing up apprenticeship of body, mind, and soul in the Shaolin way. One scene that is etched in my memory is when Kwai Chang finishes his apprenticeship. In what I take to be the final ritual of assuming the monk's status, he approaches a red-hot cauldron of coals. On the outside of the cauldron, in relief, are a dragon, on one side, and a tiger on the other. Kwai Chang readies himself, rolls up the sleeves of his robe and embraces the red-hot figures, thereby burning them onto the inside of his arms. His final passage was to embrace the pain and suffering of life because that's the Shaolin way.

It seems to me that in the Christian story, God embraces the beauty and joy and pain and suffering of the world. This is the nature of God consistently displayed in each of the "four great self-givings" (self-sacrifices) that we remember in the Christian story. In Creation, Incarnation, Passion, and Resurrection, God is displaying self-sacrifice in order to embrace life and bring new life. In Creation, God, full of life, literally explodes life, creating the universe. In the Incarnation, God empties self and becomes a human being. In the passion of Jesus, God's love goes the distance in embracing suffering. And in the Resurrection, the self-giving love of God overcomes even death to continue to bring new life.

In Week Three of *The New Spiritual Exercises,* written by Louis Savary, we see Jesus displaying, in his passion and death, the self-giving nature of God's love. As Savary puts it, "Ignatius asks us to see how Jesus on the cross identifies with wounded creation, and accepts the task of reparation, healing and transforming the damage we have been doing to ourselves and our planet" (*The New Spiritual Exercises* pp155). What we'll see is nothing less than the alchemy* of love, as God in Jesus embraces suffering, his own and the world's, in order to transform it and redeem it. (*Alchemy: a power or process of transforming something common into something special; an inexplicable or mysterious transmuting.)

Jesus embraces suffering in order to transform it. Is this "good news?" We wish suffering wasn't even a part of life, especially when it hits close to home. Often, we want our faith to be more magical so that it takes away suffering rather than be the mystery that embraces it. Wish all we want, our Christian faith isn't meant to be magical. It makes a tremendous difference in how we live. It empowers us. It sustains us. It opens the doors to possibility. But it doesn't protect us from the sufferings of life. It doesn't guarantee us instant or inevitable success. It doesn't hold back the ravages of aging. And yet, we believe Jesus has overcome suffering, transformed suffering, and even come to victory via suffering. I like the way Methodist Bishop William Willimon says it: "The Lord's Supper is not some magical medicine we take to exempt ourselves from the hard facts of life in this world. But it can provide a way of dealing with those hard facts. No prayers of a TV evangelist, no 'prayer cloth' from Arizona, no holy oil, no holy water, no holy food exempts us from the possibilities of pain, sickness, injustice, or death. To seek such exemption is to cease to follow the way of Christ.

"But at the table, before the altar, even our most painful times are redeemed because our Lord saves through suffering. The self-giving of God in Christ in the sacraments is a self-giving unto death.

"As a friend lay in her hospital bed, her body wracked by the last stages of terminal cancer, she said to me through her pain, "I couldn't take it except that I know that he has been through this and worse before me."

"Therein is our hope. Without the Cross, our faith wouldn't be a comfort to anybody. What would you say to the terminal cancer victim? What would you say to the mother of a starving child in Ethiopia? What would you say to the eighty-year-old resident of a shoddy nursing home for the elderly? 'Smile, God loves you!' No, I hope not.

"You can say that our God has been there before, in the pain, in the darkness, in the death, that Christ has come through it and that all is well" (*Sunday Dinner*, pp89).

Suffering and the Cross

The meaning of Jesus' suffering has been interpreted across the centuries in many ways and codified into doctrines of the Cross. Dr. Edward Bauman, one-time adjunct professor of Systematic Theology at Wesley Theological Seminary in Washington, D.C., wrote a study for United Methodists entitled *The Life and Teaching of Jesus*. In it, he wrote about three main meanings of the Cross. He says that for the first ten centuries, most Christians held the *ransom theory of atonement*. Living in a time when conquering nations would take the defeated into exile and often demand ransom for their release, it was only natural for believers to view the Cross through that lens. God, in Jesus' death, paid the ransom to the devil for us. Bauman says, pointing to a flaw in that theory, that this implies that God is forced to bargain with the devil and then deceive the deceiver by taking it back on Resurrection. (For me, this also elevates the devil to God-like stature, as an equal to God, which in our God is One theology just isn't the case.)

Bauman goes on to say that since the eleventh century, most Christians have held to either the *substitutionary* or *moral theory of atonement*. According to the substitutionary view, human sin so dishonored God that God had to have someone to punish in order for forgiveness to be given. Since Jesus was the only perfect person, he had to die for our sins.

For me, this has never been a theory of grace but one of violence and punishment that I cannot attribute to God. I know this builds on the ancient ritual of the perfect lamb sent out to the desert to die for the people's sins; in that way, it seems understandable to adopt this viewpoint. However, what kind of God has to have "punishment" to forgive? It seems to me that humans, needing someone to pay for injustice, have projected this onto God.

The third theory that Bauman explores is the *Moral theory of atonement* in which God, who is love, acts accordingly. When sinful humans chose to kill Jesus rather than follow him, love chose to persevere. Love chose to stay the course. Love overcomes separation by an act of self-giving forgiveness.

Teilhard's Mystical View of the Cross

Pierre Teilhard de Chardin, in his mysticism, sees another dimension to the meaning of the Cross that I call the alchemical meaning. Louis Savary puts it this way in the grace we are to pray for during the Third Week of the Exercises: "I pray to comprehend Jesus' passion and death as an action where the inexpressible intensity of his consciousness absorbs not only all the energy and intensity of his personal suffering but also of all the sin, suffering, and pain of creation, past, present, and future. And he redirects it toward the goal of the mission given to him by the Father" (*The New Spiritual Exercises* pp.158-159).

Teilhard himself said that same thought this way: "The world would leap high towards God if all the sick together were to turn their pain into a common desire that the kingdom of God should come to fruition through the conquest and organization of the Earth. May all the sufferers of the Earth join their sufferings, so that the world's pain might become a great and unique act of consciousness, elevation, and union" (*Human Energy,* 1933). (see the icon at the end of this article entitled *The Darkness Did Not Overcome It* by artist Curt Gruel that depicts this statement.)

Teilhards' evolutionary mystical meaning came to life for me in 1990 at the Journey Into Wholeness Conference at the Mo Ranch Presbyterian Retreat Center in Hunt, Texas. The conference was a five-day exploration of Jungian psychology and spirituality. One of the afternoon workshops I attended that week was led by Native American Lance Crawford, Strong Eagle. At that time,

48

Crawford was an apprentice medicine man in his tradition. His workshop, *"Paths to True Truth,"* introduced several Native ceremonies and the spirituality they embodied. He also made comparisons to the Jungian perspective and his own Christian faith.

The concluding part of his workshop was the Southern Ute Sun Dance ceremony. His presentation and witness changed my understanding of the cross forever. The Southern Utes have their Sun Dance ceremony in the summer of every year. They hold the ceremony over the course of three to four days 'so that the people might live.' Crawford said that while some tribes include piercing in their ceremonies, the Ute do not. The Ute see their Sun Dance ceremony as a healing dance. Prior to the gathering of the people, extensive preparation for the dance circle is carried out, including placing a flowering tree, The Tree of Life, at the center. As the dance commences, the people and drummers gather in a circle to support, sing, drum, and encourage the dancers. The male dancers wear skirts as a symbol of balancing male and female energies, symbolizing that they cannot know the pain of childbirth. Each dancer comes into the circle carrying their own pain, as well as the pain and needs of the community. Some dance for the orphans, some for the sick, some for the poor, some for the addicted, etc. The dancers will, in their days of dance, absorb the pain of the people.

Crawford spoke of how many understood Jesus to be at the pole, the Tree of Life, dancing with them. As the drums beat, the heartbeat of the universe is present and evolves during the ritual days. The atmosphere is infused with that energy. The dancers will dance non-stop without food and water during the ceremony. As they move together around the pole, the physical forces move them beyond words. The senses accelerate until the sage and mint brought by the people become the "drink" of the dancers.

Speaking personally about his own experience as a dancer, Crawford said: "Going without sleep and food is not an issue for me. However, going without water takes me and the other dancers to the heart of the ceremony. The Ute word for the Sun Dance means, 'I stand thirsty.' More than physical thirst it represents the spiritual thirst for the needs of the people for healing. As I dance I remember that Jesus said, 'I thirst' from the cross. He thirsted for God to be all in all. And as I dance, Jesus comes and dances with me not to give me water but to dance with me until I am open to my own nourishment in the pain. As the days progress I/we move through the pain beyond the pain to where an absolute JOY comes over me/us. I call this 'going over the barrier.'

"The last morning, when the sun comes up bringing new life, all the people join us at the Tree for prayers for healing. THE PEOPLE WILL LIVE!"

At the workshop, as he spoke of Jesus dancing with him/them and how he dances with them until they go over the barrier to the JOY beyond pain and suffering, suddenly I saw: THIS IS WHAT THE CROSS IS ALL ABOUT. Jesus is joining human suffering to move us over the barrier into the Joy of new life, the new life that comes through and beyond the pain of our human condition. It is not a price to be paid for sin so that God's justice can be satisfied. It is the price that God willingly accepts and endures to move us across the barrier. As Jesus said in John 16:22 RSV, "So, you have pain now, but I will see you again, and your hearts will rejoice, and no one will take your joy from you."

The Darkness Did Not Overcome It , Curt Gruel

Summary of Part Two

In order to fashion and understand the Christian faith story and what it means to follow the way of Jesus, it will be helpful to remember these 'lenses that help us see more clearly.'

1. None of us will ever know all there is to know of God, and we are called to always be humble and express what we hold to be true.
2. It is important to understand the place of the Bible in our faith development.
    a. It is not God's Word that is entirely literally true and factual.
    b. Jesus is God's Word and all beliefs should be fashioned according to what he taught and embodied in his earthly life.
    c. Jesus, as a teacher/rabbi, would have approached sacred scripture from a midrash perspective.
    d. We must remember that the Bible was not spoken or written in English from the beginning. It is helpful and often crucial to take into account the Aramaic language that Jesus spoke.
3. The phrase "God's will" has different meanings. Remember, there are events that happen that God doesn't want to have happen.
4. To take the Adam and Eve story and end up

believing humankind to have fallen forever into evil and depravity is to have missed the point of that myth.

5. The heaven-hell paradigm is not the primary perspective for us to have. God, in God's goodness, would never cast us into eternal flames.

6. God does not need a perfect sacrifice in order to forgive us. Jesus' primary mission was not to be a substitutionary sacrifice.

7. The Cross is the story of how God's love is willing to sacrifice in order to love deeply and unconditionally.

With these lenses in place, we move into Part Three, where we will explore Jesus' story and see what it means to follow his way!

Key Books For Further Reading

1. Books about understanding what the Bible is all about.
   A. *Reading The Bible Again For The First Time: Taking The Bible Seriously But Not Literally*, Marcus J. Borg, HarperCollins 2001
   B. *Speaking Christian: Why Christian Words Have Lost Their Power And How They Can Be Restored*, Marcus J. Borg, HarperOne 2011
   C. *Making Sense Of The Bible*, Adam Hamilton, HarperOne 2014

D. *What Do We Do With The Bible,* Richard Rohr, CAC Publishing 2018

E. *Things Hidden: Scripture As Spirituality,* Richard Rohr, St. Anthony Messenger Press, 2008

2. Books about heaven, hell, and salvation.

   A. *Love Wins: A Book About Heaven, Hell, And The Fate Of Every Person Who Ever Lived,* Rob Bell, HarperOne 2011

   B. *If Grace Is True: Why God Will Save Every Person,* Philip Gulley and James Mulholland, HarperSanFransisco 2003

   C. *Mystical Hope,* Cynthia Bourgeault, Cowley Publications 2001

   D. *Hell, No!,* Richard Rohr, CD by Center for Action and Contemplation 2014

   E. *Hell? No!,* Paul R.Smith, (to download the booklet, see revpaulsmith.com)

PART THREE
WHO IS JESUS & WHAT IT
MEANS TO BE A FOLLOWER
OF HIS WAY!

Who Is Jesus

1.

God in the Christian tradition has been called The Trinity. This is to try to describe how we experience God. We experience God as beyond us, with us and within us. The Trinity is experienced as a personal being and the Trinity itself is a "relating." To get your mind around this, think of an atom. An atom consists of a central nucleus containing positively charged protons and neutral neurons, surrounded by negatively charged electrons orbiting in electron shells. The parts relate to each other thus creating an atom. Likewise the Trinity relates in itself. With that in mind we see God at the beginning of all things.

Before the beginning of Creation: GOD. God was dancing. "Whatever is going on in God is a flow, a radical relatedness, a perfect communion between Three—a circle dance of love. And God is not just a dancer; God is the dance itself" (Rohr/ *The Divine Dance,* pp 21*)*.

Out of this dance, also called perichoresis, came all the creation. And that creation is an evolution, an ongoing life-giving dance. In other words, the Trinity has been and will be the centrifugal force within all life and its evolution. God did not make creation and then, like an artist, remain separate from what was created. If, as Paul said: "In him we live and move and have our being" (Acts 17:28), then whatever has life has it in God, and God sustains it and moves it until that life ends. Evolution, in other words, is an ongoing act of God. The Trinity has been and will be integral to anything that springs to life. And that is in our world and other worlds of the universe. At the heart of all that has life is the Trinity.

In the words of Brother Elias Marechal of Conyers, Georgia: "The ancient Greek Fathers depict the Trinity as a Round Dance...an infinite current of love streams without ceasing, to and fro, to and fro, to and fro...gliding from the Father to the Son and back to the Father, in one timeless happening" (Rohr, *The Divine Dance,* pp. 21)*.*

2.

In telling the story of Jesus then, we begin with the Trinity for Jesus is the Trinity incarnated. Before Jesus was embodied/born in our world, he was the Logos or the Word. The gospel of John says it this way. "In the beginning was the Word (Logos in Greek), and the Word was with God, and the Word was God. He was with God in the beginning. Through him all things were made, without him nothing was made that has been made. In him was life, and that life was the light of all mankind.

"The Word became flesh and made his dwelling among us. We have seen his glory, the glory of the one and only Son, who came from the Father, full of grace and truth" (vs. 1-4 NIV First-Century Study Bible).

"The Word was first, the Word present to God, God present to the Word. The Word was God, in readiness for God from day one. Everything was created through him: nothing—not one thing—came into being without him. What came into existence was Life, and the Life was Light to live by.

"The Word became flesh and blood, and moved into the neighborhood. We saw the glory with our own eyes, the one of a kind glory, like Father, like Son. Generous inside and out, true from start to finish" (vs. 1-4, The Message Bible)

3.

So, in starting this story of Jesus, we see that the Trinity in its' dance flowed and made/makes everything that is. Everything alive is a part of the flowing dance of God. Everything that is alive has its origin in the Trinity. Theologians would name the parts God (transcendent/God beyond), Son (the Word/Logos, /God with us) and the Spirit (God within). In our human history, God interacted with the people, helping them establish communities in alignment with the nature of God and the properties of the right relationship. In our Judeo-Christian faith, these stories and precepts are contained in the sacred stories of the Old Testament.

At the right time, the Trinity decided to incarnate as a human being. The Word/Logos (also known as the Cosmic Christ) became a human being as Jesus. I love how the Jesuit Priest, Michael Moynahan, expressed this mystery:

"We (the Trinity) tried in so many ways to communicate our love. If communication is not what you say but what people hear, then what we said was warped and wrenched into distancing prescriptions that had no heart.

"You asked for food. We sent manna. You asked for drink. Water flowed from the rock. You asked for directions. Moses brought the law. And on and on. Still you grew more distant, more deaf, more blind. Memories dulled. Speech slurred. Dreams dissolved into wander dust.

"And so we did what families do when confronted with calamity. We drew straws. Shorty lost. He came to share your plight, your fight, your night, and point you toward tomorrow" (*Hearts On Fire: Praying With Jesuits*, pp. 76-77).

I will be exploring this as we go along in the story I'm telling. The mystery is that the Trinity decided to incarnate as a human being. Theologians say that the Word became flesh. How that happens is a mystery. Paul, in his letter to Philippi, put it this way, *"In your relationships with one another, have the same mind as Christ Jesus: Who, being in very nature God, did not consider equality with God something to be used to his own advantage; rather, he made himself nothing by taking the very nature of a servant, being made in human likeness"* (Philippians 2:5-7, NIV First-Century Study Bible).

"Think of yourselves the way Christ Jesus thought of himself. He had equal status with God but didn't think so much of himself that he had to cling to the advantages of that status no matter what. Not at all. When the time came, he set aside the privileges of deity and took on the status of a slave, became human! Having become human, he stayed human" (Philippians 2:5-7 The Message Bible).

This God becoming human moment became understood as a self-emptying of God. The Greek word is kenosis. How this happened is a mystery, yet I believe Jesus was the Word/Logos "emptied" to become human. In this way, Jesus was the human incarnate Trinity.

Lens #8 Jesus—Human and Divine

Growing up at Ardmore, OK, First Methodist Church, I'm sure I heard every Christmas that Jesus was the Son of God and yet born of Mary, a human mother. This made him human and divine. Yet, I related more to Jesus' humanity than his divinity. I loved that he healed people and talked to those who crossed his paths in a positive way. I liked the way he gathered friends to accompany him on his journeys as an adult. I liked his compassion and the fact that he loves me. He hungered and thirsted and rested and prayed to his Abba. All these things made him attractive and believable to me.

Some who teach alternate orthodoxy don't believe in the divinity of Jesus. They believe in his humanity and regard those who thought of him as divine as under the sway of visions. For example, these teachers say that the post-resurrection appearances were visions, not real appearances. Since my awakening to the contemplative/mystical aspects of the Christian faith in 1982, I think these authors are sincere in their teachings, and I wish that they had experienced more mystical experiences in their own lives. If they had, I believe, they would be able to see Jesus as human and divine.

Little did I know that God had in store for me an even bigger, more vivid mystical experience than I had ever had before that would acquaint me with Jesus' divine side. In his first letter to the Corinthians, Paul talked about how he had heard that Jesus, on the third day was raised. As the Message Bible puts it (I Corinthians 15:5-8), "he presented himself as alive to, Peter, then to his closest followers, and later to more than five hundred of his followers all at the same time, most of them still around (although a few have since died); that he then spent time with James and the rest of those he had commissioned to represent him; and that he finally presented himself alive to me."

The experience of Jesus presenting himself alive to me came in the season of Lent 1984 as I was engaged in the Spiritual Exercises of Ignatius. That story follows....

Meeting the Divine Christ

In the spring of 1982, I attended a week-long conference at the Kirkridge Retreat Center in Pennsylvania. The topic was "The Gentile Art of Spiritual Guidance." I thought that spiritual guidance might fit with my pastoral care duties. The conference was much more than that. The leader, John Yungblut, spoke of the Christian contemplative and mystical tradition I had never heard of. He also spoke of Christian spiritual directors who helped people develop their spiritual life with God. I had never heard of them either, but on returning home I inquired and found out that the Benedictine Sisters in Oklahoma City offered such services. So, I started spiritual direction with Sister Marie

Leucke, meeting with her once a month to talk about my spiritual life with God.

After being in spiritual direction for a year, I asked Sister Marie if she knew someone who could lead me through the Spiritual Exercises of Ignatius. Many of the books I was reading kept mentioning how vital the exercises could be for one's spiritual growth. I thought I would like to do them too. Marie, as she often did, got that little gleam in her eye and smile on her face. "Bob, we Benedictines are the keepers of the Exercises for this area of the world. I would be happy to lead you through the Exercises if you want me to."

The Spiritual Exercises of Ignatius are a nine-month guided prayer journey through the life of Jesus. They highlight certain spiritual themes that had been revealed to Ignatius. Those insights led him to create the prayer journey of the exercises in the 1500s. Later, when he founded the Jesuits within the Catholic Church, they became the signature foundation of Jesuit theology and spirituality. Into these exercises, I walked in the fall of 1983.

The exercises in their retreat in daily life form require retreatants to pray every day, six days a week, on certain themes. Many of the prayers are scripture-centered. They unfold in four movements, called *Weeks* by Ignatius. Doing the exercises with Marie, I would pray during the week and then meet with her for an hour each week to talk about what had happened. Then, she would give me the next week's prayer sheet.

Jesus had been important to me for most of my life; I viewed him as a unique human being and focused on his humanity. This fit wonderfully with my dedication to pastoral care and counseling. I was trying to relate on behalf of God like Jesus related to those he came in touch with. I knew in my mind that he was thought to be fully human and fully divine, but the human side of Jesus was the side that, experientially, I was most familiar with. Shortly after the first of the year in 1984, the themes of the exercises were focusing on the events of Jesus' life. One week in particular had me praying with several scriptures that depicted the "miracles" of Jesus, e.g., calming the sea, walking on water, healings, and casting out demons, to name a few. I began to see that he might be more than I ever thought.

Over those six days, I contemplated the divine nature of Jesus and his miracles. I always ended my prayer time by being quiet with God. Then, I'd ask God:

"Did Jesus really walk on water?"

"Could he really calm the seas and weather?"

"Did he really heal people or was that just psychosomatic healing?"

"Did he really feed the five thousand?"

Each day, I had a sense that God answered me in this way, "Bob, I created the universe, if I wanted to, could I have Jesus walk on water?" "Yes, God, if you wanted to you could because you are all powerful."

Day after day, I asked and each time God answered in that way. At the end of the last question and answer time a light began to shine in the room I was praying in. A brilliant light took form and at the center of that brilliant light was a human face, the face of Jesus in all his godliness and glory. He didn't say anything to me; he just "shined," brilliantly shined. All of a sudden, I felt like 10,000 champagne bottles had uncorked in the soles of my feet and those bubbles of energy began to move all the way up and through me. They rearranged my cells in some way I cannot describe. I WAS MEETING THE DIVINE CHRIST. HE APPEARED TO ME.

After that prayer period, I was visibly shaken. I wondered if I was going crazy. Could that have really happened? Yes, it had. HE APPEARED TO ME AND HIS LIGHT HAD MOVED THROUGH ME!

I left and went home. In my car, I turned on the radio and there was some praise Jesus music playing. I began to cry. I was indeed going crazy; I hated this type of music. Simply hated it, and yet, there I was, crying because I had met him.

I told my wife, Marcy, what had happened and that I thought I was going crazy. If she thought that too she didn't say. She asked me to tell her about it. I did. Her suggestion was that I should call my spiritual director and talk with her about what had happened. When I met with Marie, she suggested that instead of feeling crazy, perhaps I could feel incredibly blessed. After all, this kind of thing didn't happen to many. Perhaps Jesus had given me an incredible gift that he knew I needed.

I took her suggestion. I let the experience be, unjudged, within me. I was changing. And I could never have guessed what that blessing was going to open up for me on my journey, which was a good thing. Better that God be in charge than me. For sure.

What Is Jesus' Mission?

To Serve the People as the Anointed One!

As Luke writes in his gospel, "Jesus returned to Galilee in the power of the Spirit, and news about him spread through the whole countryside. He was teaching in their synagogue, and everyone praised him.

He went to Nazareth, where he had been brought up, and on the Sabbath, he went into the synagogue, as was his custom. He stood up to read, and the scroll of the prophet Isaiah was handed to him. Unrolling it, he found the place where it is written: "The Spirit of the Lord is on me, because he has anointed me to proclaim good news to the poor. He has sent me to proclaim freedom for the prisoners and recovery of sight for the blind, to set the oppressed free, to proclaim the year of the Lord's favor."

Then he rolled up the scroll, gave it back to the attendant, and sat down. The eyes of everyone in the synagogue were fastened on him. He began by saying to them. "Today this scripture is fulfilled in your hearing" (Luke 4:14-21 NIV: First-Century Study Bible).

The Message Bible puts it a little differently. "Jesus returned to Galilee powerful in the Spirit. News that he was back spread through the countryside. He taught in their meeting places to everyone's acclaim and pleasure. As he always did on the Sabbath, he went to the meeting place. When he stood up to read, he was handed the scroll of the prophet Isaiah. Unrolling the scroll, he found the place where it was written, "God's Spirit is on me; he's chosen me to preach the Message of good news to the poor, sent me to announce pardon to prisoners and recovery of sight to the blind, to set the burdened and battered free, to announce, "This is God's time to shine!"

He rolled up the scroll, handed it back to the assistant, and sat down. Every eye in the place was on him, intent. Then he started in, "You've just heard Scripture make history. It came true just now in this place" (Luke 4:14-21 The Message Bible).

In his Bible Commentary, *Luke For Everyone,* N.T. Wright comments on this passage: "Why then did Jesus begin his address with the long quotation from Isaiah (61:1-2)? The passage he quotes is about the Messiah. Throughout Isaiah there are pictures of a strange 'anointed figure' who will perform the Lord's will. But, though this text goes on to speak of vengeance on evildoers, Jesus doesn't quote that part, instead he seems to have drawn on the larger picture in Isaiah which speaks of Israel being called to be the light of the nations, a theme which Luke has already highlighted in chapter 2. The servant-Messiah has not come to inflict punishment on the nations, but to bring God's love and mercy to them. And that will be the fulfillment of a central theme in Israel's own scriptures.

"This message was, and remains shocking. Jesus' claim to be reaching out with healing to all people, though itself a vital Jewish idea, was not what most first-century Jews wanted or expected. As we shall see, Jesus coupled it with severe warnings to his own countrymen. Unless they could see that this was the time for their God to be gracious, unless they abandoned their futile dreams of a military victory over their national enemies, they would suffer defeat themselves at every level-military, political and theological." (pp.48-49)

To Build the Kingdom of God on Earth

The disciples asked Jesus to teach them to pray. In what he taught, we find another dimension of his mission.

> *He said to them, "When you pray, say:*
>
> *Father, hallowed be your name,*
>
> *Your kingdom come.*
>
> *Give us each day our daily bread.*
>
> *Forgive us our sins, for we also forgive everyone who sins against us.*
>
> *And lead us not into temptation."*

Luke 11: 2-4, NIV First-Century Study Bible

The Gospel of Matthew says it a bit differently:

> *"This, then is how you should pray:*
>
> *Our Father in heaven,*
>
> *hallowed by thy name,*
>
> *your kingdom come, your will be done,*
>
> *on earth as it is in heaven.*
>
> *Give us this day our daily bread.*
>
> *And forgive us our debts, as we also have forgiven our debtors.*
>
> *And lead us not into temptation, but deliver us from the evil one.*

Matthew 6: 9-13 NIV: First-Century Study Bible

Lest we don't forget the lens of the language Jesus spoke, i.e. Aramaic. Here's one possible translation:

O Birther! Father-Mother of the Cosmos,

Focus your light within us—make it useful"

Create your reign of unity now-

Your one desire then acts with ours, as in all light, so in all forms.

Grant what we need each day in bread and insight.

Loose the cords of mistakes binding us, as we release the strands we hold of others' guilt.

Don't let surface things delude us, but free us from what holds us back.

From you is born all ruling will, the power and the life to do,

The song that beautifies all, from age to age it renews.

Truly-power to these statements-may they be the ground from which all my actions grow. Amen

Prayers of the Cosmos, Neil Douglas-Klotz, HarperSanFrancisco, 1990

Jesus, in his prayer, spoke of honoring God and God's ways. He understood his mission and that of his disciples as building the kingdom of God and helping God's peoples have what they need physically and spiritually and communally. Given what we have already learned about heaven and hell, it is noteworthy that Jesus spoke of his mission as helping us bring God's Kingdom here on earth. It's not that being with God in heaven isn't important but that we are to be about being disciples who help God's rule/reign/kingdom be here and now.

What about this idea of judgment? Didn't Jesus say he came to bring judgement? Wasn't that a part of his mission?

It's important that we clarify what might be confusing. In John's gospel Jesus says, "For judgment I have come into this world, so that the blind will see and those who see will become blind" (NIV: First-Century Study Bible). However, in John 12:47 Jesus says, "If anyone hears my words but does not keep them, I do not judge that person. For I did not come to judge the world but to save the world" (NIV: First-Century Study Bible).

How do we make sense of those two scriptures? Let's see how The Message Bible interprets his words: The Message Blble translates John 9:39 like this: "I came into the world to bring everything into the clear light of day, making all the distinctions clear, so that those who have never seen will see, and those who have made a great pretense of seeing will be exposed as blind." And in John 12:47 The Message Bible translates, "If anyone hears what I am saying and doesn't take it seriously, I don't reject them. I didn't come to reject the world; I came to save the world. But you need to know that whoever puts me off, refusing to take in what I'm saying, is willfully choosing rejection."

Too often we think of God's judgment as condemning us to punishment, but in Jesus' frame of reference judgment is to teach us to come into the light. It's like a carpenter's plumb-bob. A plumb-bob is a weight, suspended from a string. The carpenter puts the string up to the wall  so that the weight can hang down. This shows the straightness of whatever is being measured. It is not to "judge" the wall for punishment but to ascertain what needs to happen to make the wall straight and in balance.

So, Jesus' judgment is meant to show us where we have missed the mark and how to realign ourselves with the values and character of God. Of course we can reject the markers/model and close ourselves off from the relationship with Jesus but we will always be in the divine milieu and God will always be waiting to welcome us home and help us be aligned. As Paul said, "For in him we live and move and have our being" (Acts 17:28) and "nothing can separate us from the love of God that is in Christ Jesus" (Romans 8:38-39).

In John chapter 20 Jesus says that he is the good shepherd: "Very truly I tell you, I am the gate for the sheep. All who have come before have been thiefs and robbers, but the sheep have not listened to them. I am the gate, whoever enters through me will be saved. They will come in and go out, and find pasture. The thief comes only to steal and kill and destroy. I have come that they may have life, and have it to the full" (John 10:7-10 NIV: First-Century Study Bible).

Jesus came to show us how much God loves us. He came to bring us to fullness of life, both now and eternally. In his teachings, his actions, his relationships he was showing us God! And he calls all of us to be his sheep, to help him bring the kingdom on earth. Never forget that ALL means all. Jesus is always going out to bring the stray and lost sheep home. Always!

What Does It Mean to Follow the Way of Jesus?

Lois Tverberg and Ann Spangler, in their book *Sitting At The Feet of Rabbi Jesus,* explain that following a rabbi was more than absorbing lectures. It literally meant following the rabbi by traveling with him and watching not only what he taught but how he lived and carried himself. The rabbi was showing them how to live their daily lives.

Tverberg says that thinking of following as simply learning certain beliefs about God is approaching the gospel as primary information. "Being a disciple and following the way of the rabbi involves not just information but transformation. God's goal isn't to fill the world with people who believe the right things. It is to fill the world with people who shine with the brilliance of Christ" (*Sitting At The Feet of Rabbi Jesus: How The Jewishness of Jesus Can Transform Your Life,* Ann Spangler & Lois Tverberg, 2009, pp.68-69).

As an example, let's look at the great commandment. Thomas Hart, in his book *The Art of Christian Listening* (Paulist Press 1980), reflects on this central teaching of Jesus that he would expect his followers to embody. "One of the teachers of the law asked Jesus, 'Of all the commandments, which is the most important?' 'The most important one,' answered Jesus, 'is this, Hear, O Israel: The Lord our God, the Lord is one. Love the Lord your God with all your heart, and with all your soul, and with all your mind, and with all your strength. The second is this: Love your neighbor as yourself.' There is no commandment greater than those" (Mark 12:28-31 NIV: First-Century Study Bible).

In reflecting on this, Thomas Hart says: "No one will say this program is easy, but it is certainly not complicated. It demands everything of us, all day every day, but the content of the demand is basic and clear. It's as if Jesus surveyed the religious scene of his day and said to himself: These are good people, but they are all confused. They think God wants religious services, tithes, and the strict observance of the law. In fact, he wants their hearts. They think God wants religiosity, complete with sackcloth and a daily regimen. He would much rather see them love one another and share what they have with one another, so that everybody has life. They think he wants them to reject the world and isolate themselves from it, when in fact he wants them to enjoy it and give thanks for it, and to work to make it more humane. They think he wants them to live in fear, fear of going wrong and fear of him, when in fact he wants them to live in joy and freedom. They think he wants them to walk about with their heads down because of all their failures, when in fact he wants them to trust like children in his forgiveness and dependability of his love. They think they have to earn their way with him and win a reward if they can, when in fact he wants them to accept his acceptance of them as a gift quite underserved" (*The Art of Christian Living,* Thomas N. Hart, Paulist Press, 1980, pp.39).

What Are His Core Teachings?

What Jesus taught has a universal element and a particular element. The universal element relates to what the Trinity has always been about in the universe. So, Jesus was expressing God's actions in the movements of his life. In his birth, life, death and resurrection, he embodies what God has always been about.

The Universal Aspects

Birth—God has always been involved in our world and the universe. Everything that lives in the divine milieu of God. We are all born from the divine.

Life on earth—In his actions and spoken words he was revealing the nature of God. His particular human expression showed us God.

Death—God's love is willing to go all the way for us. God has always been available to help us in our suffering.

Resurrection—The resurrection of Jesus is not just for him. His resurrection expresses the truth that God brings new life out of death. It is for us all!

The Particular Aspects

These core teachings come from the four gospels, Matthew, Mark, Luke, and John except the Ten Commandments are from the Old Testament.

1. Jesus taught and embodied the character and actions of God.
   i.   God is a healing God
   ii. God's love has no limits
   iii. God is always inviting and including outsiders
   iv. God hurts for those in need

v.   God has become human in order to serve us
vi. God is about salvation and forgiveness
vii. God is about setting prisoners free
viii. God is about lifting burdens
ix. God's love is generous and gracious towards us
x.   God wants to give us good things
xi. God is trustworthy
xii. God takes the initiative toward the lost
xiii. God is like the waiting father in the parable of the Prodigal Son (Lk 15:11ff)
xiv. God's love goes all the way, even to the point of embracing suffering
xv. God is self-revealing in Jesus
xvi. In Jesus, God came to help us, to put the world right again
xvii. In Jesus, God gives us the bread of life and living water to feed our souls
xviii. In Jesus, God gives us light
xix. In Jesus, God is giving us resurrection and new life
xx. God is beyond us, within us, and with us

2. Jesus embodied and taught the character and actions of fully alive people living the values of the kingdom.
   i. Be salt. Be light
   ii. Don't say anything you don't mean

iii. Live generously and graciously toward others

iv. Don't hoard treasures

v. Judge not that ye be not judged

vi. Whatever you want people to do for you- take initiative and do it for them

vii. Live in the unforced rhythm of grace

viii. Live freely and lightly

ix. Have a flexible heart rather than an inflexible religion

x. Be childlike

xi. Be forgiving

xii. If you want to be great then serve others

xiii. Love God, love yourself, love others as yourself

xiv. Walk the talk, in other words, whatever you believe live it. As St. Ignatius of Antioch said: "We recognize a tree by its fruit and we ought to be able to recognize a Christian by their action. The fruit of faith should be evident in our lives, for being a Christian is more than making sound professions of faith. It should reveal itself in practical and visible ways. Indeed, it is better to keep quiet about our beliefs and live them out, than to talk eloquently about what we believe but fail to live by it" St. Ignatius of Antioch (35-107 AD)

xv.	Feed the hungry, give drink to the thirsty, make room for the homeless
xvi.	Clothe the shivering, visit the sick and those imprisoned
xvii.	Giving, not getting is the way; generosity begets generosity, while stinginess begets impoverishment
xviii.	Take risks of faith
xix.	Be a person whose heart breaks when others don't have what they need
xx.	Relate to all sorts of human beings, especially those who are left out
xxi.	Celebrate life, live well and blessed
xxii.	Don't run from suffering, embrace it
xxiii.	Live wide-eyed in wonder and belief so your body will be filled with light
xxiv.	Don't be bluffed into silence by religious bullies
xxv.	Resist your own greediness
xxvi.	Simply be yourself
xxvii.	Be sure to count the cost of your commitments
xxviii.	Be honest
xxix.	Pray without ceasing
xxx.	Persevere in love and faith
xxxi.	See people, engage people, listen to people, try to meet their needs
xxxii.	Trust God!

xxxiii. Follow the Ten Commandments—Be one who loves God above all. Worship no idols. Refrain from irreverent use of God's name. Keep the Sabbath holy by ceasing your striving (remember though that Jesus taught that good can be done on the Sabbath). Respect your father and mother. Don't commit murder, adultery, theft, lying, or coveting of what others have

From his Sermon on the Mount came the Beatitudes. "You are blessed when:

*You are poor in spirit, i.e., being aware that you need God's help more than anything else. This frees you from the rule of fear.

*You become sensitive to the pain and losses of those around you as well as your own

*You are meek, i.e., one who disciplines themselves to be gentle rather than harsh, nonviolent rather than violent

*You are hungering and thirsting for righteousness, i.e., living as a right-living person armed with virtue

*You are merciful, i.e., one who is tender, kind, gracious, self-giving, and loves unconditionally

* You are pure in heart, i.e., one with an undivided

heart living in awareness, watchfulness, faith, hope, and love

* You are a peacemaker, i.e., one who has inner peace, serenity, happiness and wholeness

*You are persecuted for a godly reason, i.e., being in trouble for living the kingdom values and willing to stand firm

NOTE: These are values to be learned and practiced over a lifetime. Perhaps it would be useful for you to look them over a bit at a time and ask yourself if you are embodying that quality/action. Choose one or two that need growth and make a plan to practice those in your everyday life. God will help you if you are sincerely wanting to grow. PROGRESS NOT PERFECTION IS THE WAY FORWARD! BEING ACTIVELY COMMITTED TO THESE KINGDOM VALUES IS "FOLLOWING THE WAY"!

How Can We Relate Personally To Him Now?

So far we've noted how the Trinity, God, incarnated in the human-divine person of Jesus. Jesus saw his mission as showing people of his day a fuller understanding of God. Like the Jewish prophets before him, he emphasized meeting the peoples' needs, especially those of the poor, oppressed, marginalized, and strangers/enemies. As a wise figure, he not only revealed the character of God but taught what it meant to be a person of character whose actions would help build the kingdom on earth as in heaven. Moreover, we've seen the importance of relating to him as a rabbi and friend. His disciples related to him before he was crucified and were invited to continue that with Christ after he was resurrected. Even now, Jesus is calling us to be his disciples and friends. Here are two statements that highlight that possibility.

"I want to say to all who are worshiping a picture of Jesus in a frame called History---to people who are beaten in their lonely toilsome effort to be like the Hero of that picture—that there is a richer experience than they have yet known. If they will sit down quietly He will come out of the picture into their life. A little faith—that kind of effortless prayer which is leaving of the heart's door upon the latch—and the Guest will come as often as you want Him, and you will be carried further than a whole year of fussy striving would take you; for He is not a ghost of the dead past, but a friend alive for evermore" (Leslie Weatherhead, *The Transforming Friendship*, Festival Books, pp41).

"...Jesus, the living master, is real, alive, intimately and vibrantly enfolding you right now. He is more present, in fact, than even your breath and your heartbeat. But to really know this presence you need to tune in to a different wavelength: to shift from your usual binary operating system to the heart frequency where this Jesus connection broadcasts" (Cynthia Bourgeault, *Wisdom Jesus,* Shambala Press, pp136).

Here are some ways to practice relating personally with Jesus:

Pray With Imagination

My relationship with Jesus in the beginning was with a presence that was unseen yet felt. I prayed to him, and I read about him. I had a picture of him in my mind that I would call forth when reading his stories. That felt presence brought the sense that he, indeed, was with me. Many years later, I was listening to a guided imagery prayer tape. The voice invited us to walk on a beach. I did so, imagining myself walking and taking in the smells, sights, and sounds. At one point, I noticed a piece of driftwood, and when I got to it, I bent down and picked it up. Much to my surprise, as I lifted that driftwood, it turned into the arm of Jesus shaking my hand. There he was, appearing to me without my having to conjure the image up. We walked and talked for a while. For months after that, I started my prayer times going to that beach and walking with him and talking with him. What a delight. Then, one day, he told me that he wouldn't be there for a while. He said that God wanted me to just sit quietly in God's presence. A different kind of prayer but nonetheless in the presence of the Holy.

The use of the faculty of our imaginations can help us have a deeper experience with Jesus. You may have been told that what is imaginary is not real, but that is not so. Our imagination can take us places our figuring-out mind can not go. Practice imagining yourself with Jesus.

Ignatius of Loyola, the founder of the Jesuits in the Catholic tradition, taught his students to take a scripture story and rather than reading and thinking about it, place yourself in the story. Be an extra person in the scene, watching it unfold. Perhaps you will be drawn to talk to one or more of the people in the story. Perhaps you will want to journal about your experience.

Pray With a Picture of Jesus

The picture on the next page is one I use when I need help or rescuing from burdening situations. Jesus' hand reaching out for mine brings freedom from anxiety. At other times, I use different pictures of Jesus to think about him. I have a picture of him in a fishing boat talking to the disciples. I have one of him surrounded by children. Each picture represents a different aspect of him and his life.

(If you go to revpaulsmith.com, you will find a wealth of resources about Jesus. Click on resources and then click on images of Jesus. He has over 200 images of Jesus in his collection. That may help you find some favorite ones)

Listen to Music About Jesus

When I'm feeling down, I listen to *Keep Your Eyes On Me* by Tim McGraw and Faith Hill. The song is from the soundtrack of the movie *The Shack*. I have printed out the words and read them as they sing. You can find the song online, of course. Another song I love is *Christ In Me Arise* by Trevor Thomson. It lifts my spirits. Over time, I have collected many songs that can put me in the presence of Jesus for a variety of feelings and needs.

Pray a Breath Prayer

(A breath prayer is a prayer that incorporates a word or phrase with the rhythm of your breathing. For example, if the phrase is "Breathe in me breath of God, Fill me with life anew," as you breathe in say to yourself, "Breathe in me breath of God" and upon exhaling say to yourself, "Fill me with life anew." Keep that rhythm going for a period of time. For longer phrases you'll need to divide the words into shorter statements.)

One of my favorite breath prayers I learned from Buddhist monk Thich Nhat Hanh. I use it for times of anxiety. I have changed it to fit the Christian faith.

Breathing in I calm my body
Breathing out I smile (you have to smile)
Dwelling in the present moment
I know this is a Christ filled moment.

Breathing in and through feelings helps to soften the impact and help me relax.

Another breath prayer I use when I want to feel connected to Jesus comes from Rev. Dr. Flora Wuellner. In her book *Prayer, Stress and Our Inner Wounds,* she includes this breath prayer entitled Prayer of the Heart.

Place both hands, palms down, over your heart. Rest them there for a minute or two as you relax. Then say to yourself: "The living heart of Jesus Christ is taking form with my heart...filling...calming...restoring...bringing new life. And this new life in my blood flows peacefully, with full healing power through my whole body. And the power of this new life flows into my actions and relationships with others this day. Thank you God for this grace in me" (pp23).

Talk With Jesus About Your Life Circumstances

When my late wife, Marcy, was battling cancer, someone asked me, "How is she doing?" I said, "Fine." I don't remember if that person was someone I would have shared details with, but as I reflected on my answer, it became evident to me that I didn't know how she was doing.

I wondered what I would need to know to really know how someone, myself included, is doing. Here's what I decided.

1. What has been the high point of their day/week? How did they feel about that and what did it mean to them?
2. What has been the low point of their day/week? How did they feel about that and what did it mean?
3. What are they looking forward to? How do they feel about it and what does it mean to them?
4. What are they dreading? How do they feel about it and what does it mean?
5. If someone asked them/me what I need prayer for how would they/I answer?

Practice Noticing God's Touch in Your Life Each Day

Moses was tending the flock of Jethro, his father-in-law, the priest of Midian, and led the flock to the far side of the wilderness and came to Horeb, the mountain of God. There, the angel of the Lord appeared to him in flames of fire from within a bush. Moses saw that though the bush was on fire, it did not burn up. So Moses thought, "I will go over and see this strange sight—why the bush does not burn up." When the Lord saw that he had gone over to look, God called to him from the bush, "Moses, Moses!' And Moses said, "Here I am." "Do not come any closer," God said. "Take off your sandals, for the place you are standing is holy ground" (Exodus 3: 1-5 NIV First-Century Study Bible).

Using this story as a metaphorical guide, here's a way to notice where God could have been calling to you during your day. Ask yourself these questions:

1. What happened today that I don't want to forget or can't forget? What caught your attention?
2. How might God be calling to me? What message would God want me to have from that experience?
3. How should I respond?
4. This reflection might help you notice God-moments that you might have missed.

Find a Spiritual Companion/Guide to Talk to About Your Spiritual Journey

The ancient Christian art of spiritual guidance is said to have originated with the desert fathers and mothers. They felt the call to leave the city and live in the desert and devote their time to prayer and meditation. Many seekers would come to them and ask for help.

A modern-day spiritual director/companion is trained to listen deeply to your story and assist you in learning how to notice and respond to God's activity in your life. Their task is not to tell you what to do but rather how to develop your own spiritual life so that you can discern God's leading.

You can also request information and a referral to a spiritual director by going to HeartPaths DFW (Click Spiritual Direction and then Contact Us) or going to

HeartPaths OKC (Spiritual Direction & Training | Oklahoma (the Oklahoma Branch) and click spiritual direction and then Spiritual Director Referral).

Part Three Summary

1. The Trinity created and continues to create our evolving universe. Everything lives in the divine milieu.
2. Jesus has a universal aspect, given that he came from the Trinity into human life. The universal pattern of our lives is shown in his Birth-Life-Death-Resurrection-New Life.
3. The particular aspect of Jesus is the actions and teachings as a guide for our earthly life.
4. Jesus is human and divine. One historical person said, "He became human so that we could become divine."
5. Jesus' mission is to be the anointed one described in Isaiah 61:1-2, to build the kingdom with us here on earth, to bring a judgment that leads to transformation rather than punishment, and to bring us the fullness of life that God desires for us.
6. To follow the way of Jesus is to develop your character into what God values: give hospitality to outcasts and undesirables and those on the fringes. God wants us to walk the talk and not just believe the right things.

7. Jesus saw the divine in every person. He chastised the religious leaders of his day who were taking advantage of their position and hindering people from being close to God.
8. Jesus showed us the unconditional loving nature of God.
9. Jesus is alive and present to us and wants to be our friend.
10. Several spiritual formation practices can help us attune to the heart wavelength of Jesus.

KEY BOOKS FOR FURTHER READING

1. Books about Jesus' life
   i. Jesus: A Gospel, Henri Nouwen, Orbis Books, 2001
   ii. A Portrait of Jesus, Joseph F. Girzone, image Books, 1998
   iii. Meeting Jesus Again For The First Time, Marcus Borg, HarperCollins, 1994
   iv. Sitting At The Feet of Rabbi Jesus: How the Jewishness of Jesus Can Transform Your Faith, Spangler & Tverberg, Zondervan, 2009
   v. The Evolution of Faith: How God Is Creating A Better Christianity, Philip Gulley, HarperOne, 2011
2. Books about people who made the transition from traditional to alternative orthodoxy
   i. Bitten By A Camel, Kent Dobson, Fortress Press, 2017
   ii. A Spiritual Evolution, John MacMurray, Open Table Press, 2018
   iii. Velvet Elvis, Rob Bell, Zondervan, 2005
   iv. Leaving Church, Barbara Brown Taylor, HarperOne, 2006

3. Books about alternative orthodoxy
    i. Eager To Love: The Alternate Way of Francis of Assisi, Richard Rohr, Franciscan Media, 2014
    ii. Listening To The Heatbeat of God, J. Philip Newell, Paulist Press 1997
    iii. The Divine Dance: The Trinity and Your Transformation, Richard Rohr, Whitaker House, 2016
    iv. The Universal Christ, Richard Rohr, Convergent Books, 2019
    v. The God We Never Knew: Beyond Dogmatic Religion to a More Authentic Contemporary Faith, Marcus Borg, HarperSanFrancisco, 1997
    vi. Integral Christianity: The Spirits' Call To Evolve, Paul R. Smith, Paragon House, 2011
    vii. Is Your God Big Enough, Close Enough, You Enough, Paul R.Smith, Paragon House, 2017
4. Books about Jesus' teachings
    i. The Ladder of the Beatitudes, Jim Forest, Orbis Books, 1999
    ii. Wisdom Jesus, Cynthia Bourgeault, Shambala, 2008
    iii. Prayers of the Cosmos: Meditations on the Aramaic Words of Jesus, Neil Douglas-Klotz, HarperSanFrancisco, 1990

Suffering, Louis M. Savary and Patricia H.Berne, Paulist Press, 2015

NOTE: Any book by Rob Bell, Richard Rohr, Marcus Borg, Brian McClaren, J. Philip Newell, Philip Gulley, Matthew Fox, and Louis Savary is worthy of reading in the vein of alternative orthodoxy. Also, Paul R. Smith has a website with great info about Jesus, including over 200 pictures of Jesus he collected and where you can find his *Hell, No!* in the downloadable version.

About the Author

Rev. Dr. Bob Gardenhire III, founding director of the HeartPaths Training Program in Spiritual Direction in Oklahoma City and Dallas-Fort Worth, has spent his professional life helping people discover, heal, and positively transform their lives. Whether in his role as a Methodist minister, pastoral care chaplain, psychotherapist, or spiritual director, his passion is to foster closeness to God and the formation of a richer, deeper spiritual life.

www.ingramcontent.com/pod-product-compliance
Lightning Source LLC
Chambersburg PA
CBHW051222120626
46547CB00013B/1471